Bilston

on old picture postcard

Eric Woolley

Town Hall, Bilston

1. Bilston Town Hall stands on the corner of Lichfield and Church Street. It was built in Italian style in 1872, and at one time housed the public library which opened a year later. Offices for the urban district council, the town clerk, and staff were also incorporated. The Town Hall has a tower and clock which dominates the centre of Bilston. Postcard by John Price, posted from the town in August 1907.

£2.95

Designed and Published by
Reflections of a Bygone Age
Keyworth, Nottingham
1993

ISBN 0 946245 75 4

Printed by
Adlard Print and Typesetting Services,
Ruddington, Notts.

2. A rare view of the municipal buildings in 1907. The drinking fountain which stood there for many years can be seen on the extreme right. Note the ornate gas lamp and the iron railings around the area, now used for parking. A 'boot sale' is advertised on the hoardings. Card posted from Bilston in April 1907.

LICHFIELD ST. & WELLINGTON RD., BILSTON.   No 1114.

3. The junction of Lichfield Street, Wellington Road, Walsall Street and Mount Pleasant on a postcard sent to Weston-super-Mare in September 1931. At this time there were no traffic lights and a policeman dressed in a white coat stands in the middle of the road directing what little traffic there was. A car can be seen turning into Wellington Road from Prouds Lane. Another John Price-published card.

INTRODUCTION

The Black Country town of Bilston was mentioned as long ago as 906 in Lady Wulfruna's charter, but the publication of this book marks the 60th anniversary of the town charter issued in 1933. The illustrations show the town and suburbs as it looked from the Edwardian era to the early sixties; the postcards come from a collection accumulated by my wife Wyn and myself over a period of twenty years. The large majority of the pictures have not been seen in print before.

Like most towns Bilston has undergone changes through the years: the disappearance of the old market hall, railway station, some of the shops and public houses, and even churches, has altered the area's skyline as new buildings have replaced the ones demolished. As an old industrial town, Bilston is no more, but it still retains some of its old charm and character, portrayed by these old postcards of days gone by.

The first picture postcards appeared in Britain in 1894, when Post Office regulations allowed their publication. A message could be written on the picture side of the card, with the reverse left for the address. Eight years later, this was revised to permit message and address to appear on the same side, thus leaving the whole of one side for a larger picture. A boom in buying, sending and collecting postcards followed, with publishers producing views, comic cards, greetings, and cards of famous personalities in abundance. Photographic viewcards were extremely popular, and in the Bilston area it was the firm of John Price & Sons which provided excellent coverage. Although the extended use of the telephone, increases in the price of postage, and various other factors diminished the appeal of the postcard, interesting viewcards can be found throughout this century. All these are desirable for collectors, and provide an excellent record of life in past decades.

Eric Woolley
March 1993

Front cover: A view of the Town Hall in the 1930s, taken from Swan Bank by the camera of John Price and Sons. The early trolley bus is the only traffic in the picture and is about to pass the old Lloyds Bank on the right. The card was posted from Bilston in March 1938.

Back cover (top): High Street as it looked in the fifties on a postcard by the Landscape View Publishers of Market Harborough. To the right is Dudley Street, which had a public house on each corner, the "Bull's Head" nearest the camera and the "Seven Stars" opposite. Orlando's cafe can also be seen, along with Taylor's confectionery shop on the right. Taylors also ran a milk bar and sold delicious milk shakes and icecreams.

(bottom): St. Luke's Church stood in Market Street and was built of stone in the old English style. It cost £4,825 when erected in 1852; though this included the vicarage and school buildings. In 1921 a new oak pulpit was erected as a thanks offering for peace. The church closed in the sixties and was demolished a few years later due to redevelopment of the area. Postcard by John Price & Sons.

4. Bennett Clark, the renowned Wolverhampton photographer, captured this scene looking down Wellington Road towards the Town Hall and Lichfield Street. A pony and trap, with smartly-dressed driver, waits for the photo to be taken before moving away. Walsall Street is to the right.

5. The Centre Health Clinic on the corner of Prouds Lane and Wellington Road was built in 1940. A new health centre is now operational in Prouds Lane, and the old building is used for community work.

Wellington Road, Bilston.—Winter.

6. A wintry scene of the Wellington Road with an open-topped tram trundling along the snow-covered road. This card was published by John Price and sent to Walsall in November 1905.

The Girls High School, Bilston. No 8

7. The new Girl's High School was officially opened in 1931 as the flagship of the town's educational system. Situated on Wellington Road, it is now in use as a community school.

HOLY TRINITY CHURCH, ETTINGSHALL. (Interior.)

8. Any postcard of Ettingshall is considered rare by local collectors and this one is no exception. The church was consecrated by the Lord Bishop of Lichfield on 4th December 1905. A rood screen was erected in memory of Rev. A.J.R. Haworth, who was vicar there in the twenties. Card posted at Wolverhampton in April 1908.

9. A fine photographic card by John Price & Sons showing The Crescent, which runs from Wellington Road through to Broad Street. A message on the back of the card, posted to Blackpool in August 1926 runs: *"the weather is lovely and I hope it lasts for the flower show":*

THE CRESCENT, BILSTON.

10. The war memorial at Ettingshall commemorates those who died in the 1914-18 war. Remembrance ceremonies are still conducted in November each year. Another John Price card.

11. This view of Mount Pleasant looking towards the Willenhall Road shows the Drill Hall and the old Theatre Royal on the left, and the "Globe" Hotel and police station on the right. Many famous music hall artists started their careers in smaller theatres like this; Bruce Forsyth made his stage debut here at fifteen. Sadly, the theatre was demolished in the early 1960s, and the "Globe" suffered the same fate in the following decade. The Drill Hall is still standing and has been used as a night club and comedy theatre in recent times, as well as a battalion Headquarters. *(See illus. 15)*

Willenhall Road, Bilston, shewing New Drill Hall, Theatre, &c.
John Price & Son's Picture Post Cards. No. 73.

Nº5 Mount Pleesent & Art School, Bilston.

12. View of Mount Pleasant looking towards Willenhall Road in the 1930s. Overhead trolley bus wires are visible between the trees lining the road, but the School of Art is the main feature. The foreground is totally devoid of traffic or pedestrians.

886   BILSTON GIRLS HIGH SCHOOL. STAFFS EDUCATION COMMITTEE.

13. A large building known as Brueton House on Mount Pleasant was used as the Bilston Girls High School before it was transferred to a new site on Wellington Road *(see illus. 7)*. The house is now the site of the library, art gallery and museum. John Price card, posted from Bilston in January 1925.

14. The Art and Technical Schools on Mount Pleasant, pictured here about 1931, is one of Bilston's older education facilities, used for further studies in art, science and commercial subjects; at one time special training was given to students engaged in local trades.

15. Described as a large and commodious building, the Drill Hall was the headquarters of the 6th South Staffordshire Regiment. It is now used as a comedy theatre: the cannons and iron chains were removed during the second world war.

16. A John Price postcard of about 1930 showing the new corporation housing scheme in and around Bunkers Hill Lane, which runs from Willenhall Road to Moseley Road.

17. The parish church of St. Leonards in Walsall Street dates back to 1445, where it is mentioned in letters patent for a chantry to be dedicated to the saint. The church closed down in 1536, re-opened in 1557, and was rebuilt in 1826 at a cost of £9,000. A further £2,000 was spent to encase the building in cement and rebuild the tower. The baptism and marriages register dates from 1684 and the burial register from 1716.

SWAN BANK, BILSTON

18. A look at Swan Bank in the fifties on a John Price postcard. Traffic, including cyclists, is quite dense. The "White Rose" public house is on the left, identified by its floral sign.

J. PRICE & SONS,
BILSTON

19. A stone edifice in the form of a cross constitutes the war memorial on Swan Bank and Oxford Street. The names of the fallen of both world wars are on plaques which have been renewed thanks to the efforts of the local branch of the Royal British Legion during the last few years.

20. The church of St. Mary the Virgin in Oxford Street was built in 1830 by the ecclesiastical commissioners out of what was known as the "million grant". Built of stone, it consists of chancel, nave, porch, and an eastern tower with pinnacles containing a clock and one bell. It has had several improvements and decorations over the years, notably in 1919 when a lady chapel was added.

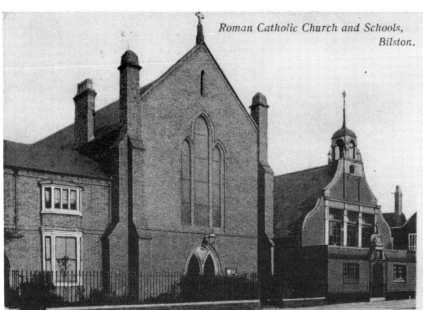

Roman Catholic Church and Schools, Bilston.

John Henry, afterwards Cardinal Newman, author of "Lead Kindly Light," laboured at Bilston during the Cholera Visitation of 1847. See Newman's "Apologia," page 370.

21. The Roman Catholic Church of the Holy Trinity was built in 1833 and enlarged eleven years later. John Henry Newman, later Cardinal Newman, and author of *"Lead, kindly light",* was stationed here for a short time and worked very hard amongst the sick and dying during the cholera epidemic of 1847.

22. Church Street on a Price postcard of about 1905, looking towards the High Street with many pedestrians and shoppers – but no traffic. The trams used to go right through the town centre and a dual set of lines can be seen here running up the middle of the highway.

23. Bilston's Market Hall was opened in 1891 – market days, established by the local market act of 1824, were Mondays and Saturdays. The hall was demolished in the early 1970s for redevelopment and a modern structure now exists for the market.

PRIMITIVE METHODIST CHURCH AND SCHOOLS, BILSTON.

24. The Primitive Methodist Church in the High Street. The church is on the left and the Jubilee Schools to the right on this early John Price postcard. The buildings disappeared in 1962 when the church was amalgamated with the Swan Bank Wesleyan to form the Bilston Methodist Church.

25. A rare glimpse of the top end of the High Street in the 1950s. The "Bird in Hand" public house is on the right, and Wolverhampton Street runs to the left through the traffic lights.The scene has completed changed now as the new Black Country route takes shape.

26. The Central School for Boys in Ashley Street was opened in 1920 and later became the Bilston Boys' Grammar School until new premises were built on a new estate which at one time was the Bilston and Willenhall golf club site.

ENTRANCE.

THE LATE SIR

Hickman

MEMORIAL FOUNTAIN.

27. Four scenes of the park plus an inset of the benefa
cards forming the montage were also printed as individ
hampton in December 1911.

THE GROTTO.

HICKMAN, BART.

rk, Bilston.

BANDSTAND.

Alfred Hickman from whom the park gets its name. The four
s by John Price & Sons. This card was posted from Wolver-

FRAZER ST. BILSTON.

28. A view of Frazer Street with its row of terraced houses on the right and a glimpse of the school, named after one of Bilston's famous sons, John Etheridge. Ashley Street is the road in the foreground. A John Price card, posted from Birmingham in April 1917.

COMMERCIAL HOTEL

PIPE HALL HOTEL

29. The "Pipe Hall" Hotel in Hall Street was probably the best-known establishment of its type in the town. The building is unrecognisable on this picture compared with today's building. The facia has completely altered and has a large open frontage at the entrance. It is now a night club and since its original form in the eighteenth century, it has undergone many changes. The Pipe Hall was once the residence of a well known Bilston family of the same name.

30. Bilston Central Railway station in the early 1960s complete with footbridge and a diesel locomotive-hauled passenger train. It was a sad day for the town when the station, on the old Great Western Line, was closed in 1971, as many people had found it a convenient way to travel to Birmingham on shopping trips.

31. Another view of the railway station looking towards Wolverhampton. The "Pipe Hall" Hotel can just be seen to the right of the bridge, and some of the old dwellings to the left, where the area has been redeveloped to accommodate the new Black Country road.

32. A rare look at the Great Western Railway goods depot about 1930, situated behind the Central railway station with its entrance in Bath Street. Two fully-loaded stationary vehicles are in the background, one with boilers probably made at the local works of John Thomsons.

33. St. Mary's Church vicarage stood in Bath Street, and was the birthplace of Sir Henry Newbolt, the famous poet, whose father was the vicar of St. Mary's when Newbolt was born in 1862. One of his best-known works was *"Drakes's Drum"*, though he wrote many seafaring poems.

34. Bilston's swimming baths in Market Street were taken over by the governing authority in 1870. They were rebuilt in 1895 and included slipper baths and a swimming pool, but are no longer there, new baths having been built in Prouds Lane to replace them.

35. The school known as Stonefield was built in 1905-6, and it looks as if the road we now know as Prosser Street had not been completed when this Price postcard was published.

36. Etheridge Road is on the Villiers estate and consisted of council-built homes. The name derives from one of Bilston's best-loved men, John Etheridge (1772-1856), who was heavily involved with Sunday Schools, helping ragged children and comforting cholera victims. His good works included giving away 10,000 bibles and 41,000 prayer books, and many of Bilston's parishioners wept when they heard of his death.

37. Another of the narrow roads around the Villiers estate was Owen Road, seen here on a 1920s card. Owen Place is just off to the left. Most of the roads in the area were named after local councillors.

1059. VILLIERS AVENUE.

38. Villiers Avenue, looking towards the Wellington Road, was once a very residential suburb of Bilston, with large bungalows and houses being erected on one side and the tennis club opposite: the club room is the building on the left. Bilston bowling club is situated on the right, but out of the picture. This part of the avenue still looks the same today. John Price 'Real Photo' series card, posted from Bilston in August 1930.

Memorial Fountain, Hickman Park, Bilston.

39. The decorative drinking fountain in Hickman Park was opened on 22nd June 1911 to commemorate the coronation of George $\underline{V}$. The schoolchildren in the background are probably enjoying a day off for the celebrations.

WESLEY CHURCH, BILSTON.

40. Methodism came to Bilston almost eighty years before the church was opened on Swan Bank in 1823. This unusual card shows two views of the old church which was demolished during the 1960s and a new building erected on the site. To the left of the top picture is what was once the Manse. This building is still standing. The church was in fact the first place in the town to use gas lighting, having use of its own supply manufactured on an adjacent site at the rear of the church.

41. An unusual card showing the pond and flower beds in Hickman Park with the drinking fountain in the background. Postally used at Bilston in April 1936, the card was produced by an anonymous publisher.

HICKMAN PARK. BILSTON.

WESLEYAN CHURCH, BRADLEY

42. Bradley was no exception to the spread of the Methodist movement in the area, and the church there was built in 1902, replacing the old one which was badly damaged by lightning during 1901. It was in the old chapel that the famed iron pulpit made by John Wilkinson was retained. Wilkinson, so it was said, was buried in an iron coffin made at his factory. No.94 in Price's postcard series. *"This church is in front of our house,"* wrote Gertie to her aunt.

St. Martin's Church, Bradley.

John Price & Sons' Picture Post Card. No. 96.

43. The Church of St. Martin in Bradley was constructed in 1866 at a cost of £6,000 and was built of stone in the early English style. The spire was a famous landmark around Bilston and could be seen from many parts of the area; sadly the church had to be demolished, but the school rooms belonging to it still stand.

44. "The Prince of Wales" in Highfield Road was one of Bradley's popular public houses, in the William Butler's group of establishments found throughout the area. This photographic card dates from around 1932.

45. A motor charabanc belonging to the Bilston Motor Services Company fully loaded for a day's outing in 1925. The company's telephone number was a double-digit 94.

46. Most factories formed their own troop of home guards during the second world war. Here is the bunch of men who formed the one from Joseph Sankey and Sons' factory at Albert Street, Bilston. Their official name was no.10 company, 34 Battalion South Staffs, Home Guard.

47. Groups of refugees who fled Belgium during the Great War were dispersed to many towns in this area and some of these who took refuge in Bilston are seen on this card. Although looking well and smartly-dressed, they appear dejected: the faces of the children seem to tell all.

48. This photographic card shows the staff from the Bilston employment exchange (or the 'Labour', as it was better-known by anyone unfortunate to lose their job and who had to sign on the dole). Note the four servicemen in their uniforms, complete with campaign medals, in the centre of the picture.

STAFFORDSHIRE CONSTABULARY. BILSTON DIVISION. April 5th, 1911.

49. A postcard published by A. Palmer of Small Heath, Birmingham, showing the Bilston division of the Staffordshire Constabulary posing for the photographer – 48 are on parade.

No. 15207

Hickmans Steel Wor

50. An aerial view of Alfred Hickman's steel works at Spring Vale. Better known as Stewart and Lloyds or British Steel to the younger people of the town, the steel works once held the European record for open-hearth steel output thanks to a huge blast furnace affectionately called Elizabeth or "Big Lizzie". The skyline of Bilston was altered dramatically with the demolition and closure of this profit-making plant, and was a

ilston, from the Air.   Aerofilms Series

huge blow to the thousands who had been employed there. The postcard by Aerofilms
of Hendon was posted at Bilston in April 1937. *(See illus. 55).*

C. 335. AERIAL PHOTOGRAPH OF PART OF WORKS AND OFFICES OF
JOHN THOMPSON LTD., ETTINGSHALL, WOLVERHAMPTON.

51. Aero Pictorial postcard of John Thompson's works at Ettingshall. The firm was established by William Thompson in 1840; he was succeeded by his son John, who died in 1909, but had been in partnership with five other members of the family. Thompsons were famous for the manufacture of boilers of all kinds, and received awards for industry, including gold medals in 1891-2 and a diploma at the Franco-British Exhibition of 1908. Gold was also awarded at the Japan-British Exhibition of 1910.

Considerable attention has been given to the utilisation of waste products in the Black Country. Our picture represents a recently erected plant at Bilston, for the manufacture of paving slabs from furnace refuse.

52. Waste-recycling in 1910. John Price's postcard caption confirms that the plant was at Bilston, but there is no clue to the actual location.

ETTINGSHALL CHURCH FOOTBALL CLUB.

53. This card of the local soccer team from Ettingshall church was sent from 20 Martin Street, Parkfields, by someone named H. Jukes about 1910. The local policeman (in the middle row in full uniform) was obviously a supporter! The team are posed to show off the trophy they have won, and the committee are dressed in their Sunday best.

54. J.E. Downs had butchers' shops and premises at 102, 108 and 110 Church Street, Bilston. He was a noted ham and bacon curer and sold sausages at the time this picture was taken from 8d per lb. This advertising card dates from about 1932.

55. A fine photographic card of Spring Vale steel works *(see illus.50)*. From 1866-84 iron was produced before owner Sir Alfred Hickman turned it over to steel making; Bilston was to become famous for its open-hearth method. It was taken over by Stewart and Lloyds in 1920, and after nationalisation the works were owned by British Steel. They were closed down in 1979.

BLAST FURNACES, NEAR BILSTON. (No. 737)

56. The blast furnaces at the steel works are featured here on a John Price photographic card of 1929.